Georgetown Elementary School
Indian Prairie School District
Aurora, Illinois

TITLE I MATERIALS

YOU CHOOSE
BOOKS ™

The Revolutionary War

An Interactive History Adventure

by Elizabeth Raum

Consultant:
Len Travers
Associate Professor of History
University of Massachusetts at Dartmouth

Capstone
press ®

Mankato, Minnesota

You Choose Books are published by Capstone Press,
151 Good Counsel Drive, P.O. Box 669, Mankato, Minnesota 56002.
www.capstonepub.com

042010
005756R

Library of Congress Cataloging-in-Publication Data
Raum, Elizabeth.
    The revolutionary war : an interactive history adventure / by Elizabeth Raum.
    p. cm. — (You choose books)
    Summary:"Describes the events of the American Revolutionary War and explains the
significance of the war today. The reader's choices reveal the historical details from the perspective
of a young girl, a patriot fighter, and a Loyalist determined to keep America under British rule" —
Provided by publisher.
    Includes bibliographical references and index.
    ISBN 978-1-4296-3420-5 (library binding)
    ISBN 978-1-4296-3912-5 (softcover)
    1. United States — History — Revolution, 1775–1783 — Juvenile literature. I. Title.
II. Series.
E208.R38 2010
973.3 — dc22   2009012552

Editorial Credits
Megan Schoeneberger, editor; Juliette Peters, set designer; Veronica Bianchini, book designer;
    Wanda Winch, media researcher

Photo Credits
Corbis/Bettmann, 26
Getty Images Inc./National Geographic/Louis S. Glanzman, 28
The Granger Collection, New York, 81
Library of Congress/Prints and Photographs Division, 10, 23, 54, 100
Military History, Smithsonian Institution, Karen Carr, artist, 43
National Parks Service/Colonial National Historical Park/Sidney E. King, artist, 6; Harpers
    Ferry Center/Keith Rocco, artist, 95
North Wind Picture Archives, 17, 40, 47, 60, 64, 68, 74, 84
Paintings by Don Troiani, www.historicalimagebank.com, cover, 12, 37
Pamela Patrick White, www.ppatrickwhite.com, 88
Pictorial Field Book of the Revolution by B.J. Lossing, 1859, 18, 35, 89
SuperStock, Inc./SuperStock, 105

TABLE OF CONTENTS

ABOUT YOUR ADVENTURE

YOU live in the American colonies in the late 1700s. Tensions between America and Great Britain are brewing. As war looms on the horizon, which side will you choose?

In this book, you'll explore how the choices people made meant the difference between life and death. The events you'll experience happened to real people.

Chapter One sets the scene. Then you choose which path to read. Follow the directions at the bottom of each page. The choices you make will change your outcome. After you finish one path, go back and read the others for new perspectives and more adventures.

YOU CHOOSE the path you take through history.

5

Colonists first settled in small towns near the Atlantic Ocean.

War Begins

In 1776, you are living in the American colonies. Like most people in America, you consider yourself British. Some people think of themselves as being from a particular colony, such as Virginia, New York, or Connecticut. You do not feel especially connected to people in the other 12 colonies, though. In fact, like most colonists, you have never traveled more than 30 miles from home.

For the last few years, tensions between the colonies and Britain's King George III have been increasing. When the French and Indian War ended in 1763, Britain was deeply in debt. The king expected the colonists to help pay for Britain's war expenses.

Turn the page.

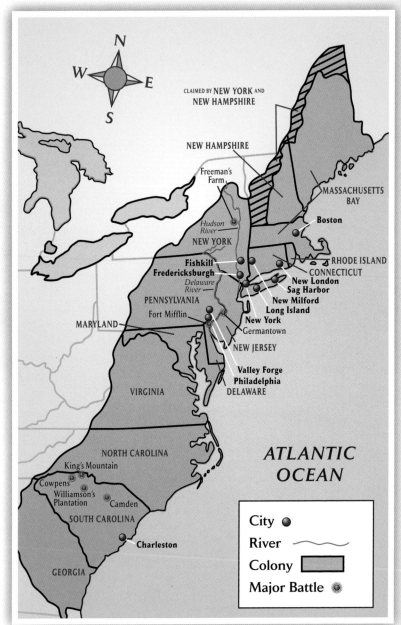

N
W   E
S

CLAIMED BY NEW YORK AND NEW HAMPSHIRE

NEW HAMPSHIRE

Freeman's Farm

MASSACHUSETTS BAY

Hudson River

Boston

NEW YORK

RHODE ISLAND

Fishkill

CONNECTICUT

Fredericksburgh

New London

Delaware River

Sag Harbor

PENNSYLVANIA

New Milford

Fort Mifflin

Long Island

MARYLAND

New York

Germantown

NEW JERSEY

Valley Forge

Philadelphia

DELAWARE

VIRGINIA

ATLANTIC OCEAN

NORTH CAROLINA

King's Mountain

Cowpens

Williamson's Plantation   Camden

SOUTH CAROLINA

Charleston

GEORGIA

City ●

River ～

Colony ▭

Major Battle ◎

In 1765, the British government passed the Stamp Act. This law taxed all printed materials, including newspapers, stamps, and playing cards. But Americans objected. They refused to accept laws made by the British Parliament.

Great Britain did not back down. Other taxes followed the Stamp Act. In 1768, troops arrived in Boston, Massachusetts, under the leadership of Major General Thomas Gage. Small fights broke out between the soldiers and the townspeople. On March 5, 1770, British soldiers fired into a crowd, killing five men. Patriot leader Samuel Adams called this the Boston Massacre.

On December 16, 1773, colonists dumped British tea in Boston Harbor rather than pay a tax on tea. This was called the Boston Tea Party. In response, Great Britain sent more troops to Massachusetts and closed the port of Boston.

Turn the page.

The other colonies defended Massachusetts. The First Continental Congress, held in Philadelphia in 1774, called on Great Britain to respect the colonists' rights.

On April 19, 1775, American militiamen and British soldiers clashed at Lexington and Concord, Massachusetts. The Americans won these first battles of the Revolutionary War. Great Britain responded by sending more troops to the colonies.

George Washington (on white horse) took charge of the Continental army in 1775.

British and American troops continued to fight. The British won a major victory at the Battle of Bunker Hill in June 1775.

On July 15, 1775, the Second Continental Congress appointed George Washington commander-in-chief of the Continental army. On July 4, 1776, Congress approved the Declaration of Independence.

People throughout the colonies have divided themselves into two groups. Patriots favor independence from Great Britain. Loyalists, also called Tories, want to remain under British rule. The time has come to choose sides. What role will you play in the war?

→ To be the daughter of a militia captain, turn to page **13**.

→ To fight as a young Connecticut patriot, turn to page **41**.

→ To remain loyal to Great Britain, turn to page **75**.

Patriots formed militias, which were groups of citizens ready to fight as soldiers in an emergency.

CHAPTER 2

Daughter of the Revolution

It's October 1776. The war with Britain is underway. In June 1776, the British lost the Battle of Sullivan's Island. Two months later, in August, the British won the Battle of Long Island. Now, British war ships are gathering off the coast of New York. More fighting seems likely.

Soldiers, traders, and supplies pass through your hometown of Fredericksburgh, New York, daily. One day, your brother Robert runs into the house. "Someone's coming," he shouts.

You rush outside as a man on horseback comes into the yard. "I've come from Fishkill with a message," he says.

Turn the page.

"Follow me," you say. You lead the way to the gristmill where your father is grinding grain into flour. Father heads the local militia regiment.

After the messenger leaves, Father says, "The militia must to go to Fishkill and guard the Hudson River."

You help pack food and supplies. Wives often go to war with their husbands, but your mother has a new baby. She cannot travel. You offer to go along. "I'm 15. I can cook and clean for you."

"You may come if you want," Father says. "But there is important work here too. Enoch Crosby, the shoemaker, is one of our spies. His information helps us fight the British. He may need help."

→ To go to Fishkill with Father, go to page **15**.

→ To stay home, turn to page **17**.

You go with Father to Fishkill. The town is headquarters for John Jay and his Committee of Safety. The committee provides leadership in the struggle for independence.

You and Father rent rooms above Mrs. Mary Bloodgood's hat shop. A few days later, Father goes to the town of White Plains. It is about 50 miles south of Fishkill. "General Washington fears there will be a British attack there," he says.

While Father is away, you stay with Mrs. Bloodgood. Father returns to Fishkill on November 4. He tells you about the Battle of White Plains. "On October 28, we fired some shots at the British. They fired back," Father says. "We thought they'd come after us, but they didn't. They marched back to New York City."

Turn the page.

"Did you meet General Washington?" you ask.

"Yes. He's a great leader," Father says. "When he speaks, men listen."

Militiamen serve for a few months at a time. By winter, you and Father go home. It's good to be with the family again. But in September 1777, you return with Father to Fishkill. General Washington orders patriots to go north and stop British General John Burgoyne and his troops. Mrs. Bloodgood suggests that Father let you stay with her. "The fighting could be heavy," she says.

➤ To go home to Fredericksburgh, go to page **17**.

➤ To go north with the militia, turn to page **24**.

➤ To stay at Fishkill, turn to page **26**.

Most colonial families lived on farms outside of cities and towns.

There's plenty to do on the farm and at your father's gristmill. Weeks and months pass quickly. You receive word that General Washington is in New Jersey. Father remains in Fishkill to guard supplies there.

One night, there's a knock at the door. It's late. You are in bed. The rest of the family is already asleep. It could be Crosby or another patriot needing help. Or it could be British soldiers.

→ To answer the door, turn to page **18**.

→ To go wake Mother, turn to page **19**.

You answer the door. It's Enoch Crosby, the patriot spy. "Quick, hide me," he whispers. "British soldiers are following me."

You want to help Crosby, but if the British find a spy in your house, they might burn it down. Maybe you should send Crosby out the back door. He can hide in the barn or the gristmill, unless the soldiers are covering the back too.

Enoch Crosby was a shoemaker who offered to spy for the patriots.

➤ *To show Crosby out the back door, turn to page **29**.*

➤ *To hide him in the house, turn to page **31**.*

You go upstairs to wake Mother, but the knocking stops. Whoever was there goes away.

A few nights later, someone knocks again. "We're the king's soldiers, and we're hungry!" they shout.

Your mother comes down the stairs. "If we don't open the door, they'll knock it down," she says.

You and your mother prepare bread and cheese for the British soldiers. "Soon we'll be eating like this every day," one soldier says.

Another soldier gives him a nudge. "Watch what you say."

"These women are no danger to the British! Neither are the rebels at Fishkill. We'll have no trouble at all," his friend says.

Turn the page.

It's after midnight when the soldiers leave.

"They plan to attack the supply depot at Fishkill," you tell your mother.

"Yes, I believe you're right," she says.

"I must find a way to warn Father."

But your mother warns you, "The woods are full of Cow Boys and Skinners."

Cow Boys and Skinners are dangerous men who often hide in the woods. Cow Boys steal supplies for the British. Skinners favor the patriots, but if they're hungry, they'll steal from anyone. Neither will stop to ask who you are. "Contact the spy network instead," Mother pleads.

➤ To go to Fishkill to find Father, go to page **21**.

➤ To contact the spy network operating in the area, turn to page **32**.

The sooner you tell Father, the better. It's a 20-mile trip through thick forests. It's late, and you have only the moon to light your way.

You saddle your horse, Blaze, and leave home. You hope the darkness will hide you from the Cow Boys and Skinners. You push Blaze to run faster.

Something smacks you in the head. It's a tree branch. You fly off Blaze. Before you can move, a boot lands on your stomach. "Stop! You're hurting me!" you cry. You grab the man's boot and twist it hard.

"Ouch!" he yells. You keep twisting until he loses his balance and falls. You leap up, run to Blaze, and race into the night. You're safe for now, but badly frightened.

→ To continue to Fishkill, turn to page **22**.

→ To circle around and go home, turn to page **32**.

You race on. The sun is rising as you arrive in Fishkill. You find your father with John Jay.

"Is something wrong at home?" Father asks.

"Everyone is fine," you reply. You warn him about the British attack.

"Good work," Jay tells you.

Father is staying in the room over Mary Bloodgood's hat shop. She offers you breakfast.

"I don't want you going home alone. It's too dangerous," Father says after you tell him about the man in the woods. "I must go north with the militia tomorrow. British General John Burgoyne is marching his troops south. If another British general, General Howe, marches north from New York City, the British will control the route up the Hudson River to Canada. They are trying to separate New England from the rest of the colonies. We must stop him."

John Jay was a member of
the Continental Congress.

"Then I'll go north with you," you say.

"Or you could stay here with me,"
Mrs. Bloodgood offers. "You'll be safer, and
I can use the help."

→ To go north with Father, turn to page **24**.

→ To stay in Fishkill, turn to page **26**.

You're eager to go north with the militia. Perhaps you can help. You walk behind the supply wagons with other women and children.

"Women are a necessary part of an army," one woman says. "We sew, cook, do laundry, and care for the sick and wounded. I've even seen women pick up a gun during battle and shoot. After all, we have to defend ourselves."

General Washington has sent militia to guard the Hudson River from Burgoyne's troops. On September 18, 1777, you camp at Freeman's Farm on the Hudson River. Scouts report that the British are camped 2 miles away.

The next morning, Colonel Daniel Morgan and his Virginia riflemen are first onto the battlefield. Other militia groups join them. You wait with the women behind the troops. It's quiet, almost eerie.

First you hear a single shot, then hundreds follow. Noise and smoke fill the air. Suddenly a soldier stumbles out of the smoke. "Help me," he calls. Blood gushes from a wound on his right arm. You rush forward and press a cloth against the wound. The bleeding slows.

Another soldier calls out, and another. You fill a bucket with water and head toward the voices.

Before you realize it, you are in the midst of the fighting. A soldier lies on the ground, bleeding. Nearby, a group of soldiers are firing a large cannon.

"Give us a hand here," a soldier calls. "We need water to cool down the cannon."

➤ To continue tending the wounded, turn to page **27**.

➤ To help cool the cannon, turn to page **37**.

Women helped the war effort by sewing clothes and blankets for the soldiers.

"I'm glad you decided to stay," Mrs. Bloodgood says. "One of the biggest needs is clothing," she explains. "You can help by sewing and washing clothes with Mrs. Woodhull. She's in charge of clothing supplies. Or you can help at the hospital. Nursing is difficult but important work."

→ *To sew clothes, turn to page* **33**.

→ *To work as a nurse, turn to page* **35**.

Someone else will have to get water. You want to help the fallen soldier. You press a cloth against his wounded arm to stop the bleeding. Then you tie a bandage around his arm.

Other soldiers call for help. Many men have gaping gunshot wounds. Others have been pierced by British bayonets.

You hold the hands of the dying. Then you move on to help others. One man cries out for his mother. You give what comfort you can. He dies with his head resting in your lap.

The fighting lasts for five hours. By the end of the day, blood soaks your dress. Smoke and tears smear your face. Soldiers carry the wounded to a medical tent and bury the dead.

"We won the battle," a doctor says. "But we lost 80 men."

Turn the page.

Some women helped wounded soldiers on the battlefields.

More than 200 Americans were wounded in the battle. Most of the wounded soldiers will be moved to a hospital in Fishkill.

"We need nurses to care for the soldiers there. Would you help?" the doctor asks.

You don't want to return to the battlefield. But nursing is such sad work. Perhaps you could help repair uniforms instead.

➤ To repair uniforms, turn to page **33**.

➤ To work at the hospital, turn to page **35**.

You don't dare hide Crosby inside the house. "Follow me," you say, checking to see that the way is clear. You lead Crosby to the mill. Once inside, you duck behind bags of flour. It should be safe here.

You hear a crashing noise. Soldiers are in the mill!

"Take this flour," one man yells. "We may not have found the spy, but at least we found supplies." The soldiers haul bag after bag of flour out of the mill into a waiting wagon. You signal to Crosby to follow you out the side door. Maybe you can escape before the soldiers notice you.

"Stop!"

They've seen you. Two men grab you, and three take hold of Crosby.

Turn the page.

"What are you doing?" Crosby says. "Can't a man visit his girl? I just wanted to say good-bye before I leave to serve for the British."

"British?" they ask.

Crosby is a very convincing liar. The men believe him. "You're welcome to the flour," Crosby says, "but there's no need to frighten a young girl." They let you go.

Once the soldiers are gone, Crosby leaves. "I'll be back," he says with a smile. "Thank you for giving me a safe place to hide."

Turn to page 39.

Crosby can hide in the house. There's a secret staircase that leads to the attic. He slips upstairs into the darkness. You blow out the candles and rush back to your bed.

Suddenly you hear more knocking. The baby cries. You, Mother, and all the other children get up. They crowd around her as she opens the door.

Two British soldiers stand there. "Sorry to bother you. But we are looking for a troublemaker."

"No one has come by here," Mother says, trying to calm the crying baby. "We were all asleep."

As soon as they leave, you tell Mother that Crosby is hiding in the attic. She smiles. "Your father will be pleased. Keep Crosby hidden until the soldiers are far away."

The next night, Crosby sneaks away to deliver his secrets to John Jay and the Committee of Safety.

Turn to page **39**.

The woods are too dangerous. The message will have to wait.

The next morning, you go to town. Mrs. Clark, who runs a small bookshop, is a trusted friend of liberty.

"Have you seen Crosby lately?" you whisper.

She takes you into the back of the store. "I can reach him." She agrees to relay your message to Crosby. "He'll get it to John Jay."

"You're one of us now," she says. You're proud that you've found a way to help win freedom.

THE END

To follow another path, turn to page 11.
To read the conclusion, turn to page 101.

You decide to repair uniforms with Mrs. Woodhull, who is in charge of the clothing supplies. "Women throughout the colonies are sewing," she says. "In Connecticut, every town has a quota of clothing they must provide to us here in Fishkill. In Hartford, for example, the women are to complete 1,000 coats and 1,600 shirts. People in other colonies are helping too."

Everything is sewn by hand. You sew all day. Then you sew by candlelight until you fall asleep.

In October, Father returns to Fishkill. "Britain's General Burgoyne surrendered at the Battle of Saratoga," he says. "I'm free to go home."

"May I stay at Fishkill to sew with Mrs. Woodhull?" you ask.

"Of course," he replies.

Turn the page.

As the war goes on, the Continental army runs out of warm coats, pants, and socks. They are out of shoes too, but you can't sew shoes.

By 1778, there's a building at Fishkill just for men who have no clothing at all. Their shirts, pants, and socks wore out, and they have no others. They cannot return to war service without clothes. Every outfit you complete means one soldier returns to battle. Some patriots fight the British with guns and rifles. You win freedom with a sewing needle.

THE END

To follow another path, turn to page 11.
To read the conclusion, turn to page 101.

Fishkill's Trinity Church was used as a hospital during the Revolutionary War.

Trinity Church becomes the hospital. Pews are moved out and cots moved in. The wounded soldiers are brought back to Fishkill.

There are hundreds of soldiers in the hospital. Many are terribly wounded. Caring for them is hard work.

Turn the page.

You help prepare the men's meals and try to make them comfortable. You wash their bodies, change bandages, and give medicine. Occasionally you help doctors remove wounded arms or legs.

Often you write letters to wives, mothers, and girlfriends. Many soldiers are too badly wounded to write themselves. They mumble the words as you write. Others don't know how to read or write. Thanks to you, their families will learn what happened. Some soldiers will live to return home, but their wounds will change their lives forever. You will always remember the patriots who gave their lives to win the war.

THE END

To follow another path, turn to page 11.
To read the conclusion, turn to page 101.

You rush to the cannon. The soldier grabs your pail of water. He dips a sponge in the water and uses it to cool the cannon. The cannon must be cooled each time it fires 10 or 12 rounds.

After the battle ends, you gather up rifles and muskets left behind on the battlefield. General Washington's troops are short of weapons, and a good musket costs more than a week's pay.

During battles, soldiers used water to keep their cannons cool.

Turn the page.

On October 17, 1777, General Burgoyne surrenders at the Battle of Saratoga. Defeating Burgoyne is a good sign for the Americans. Your father's regiment returns home. He'll go off again, but next time you'll stay home to help Mother with the farm. You were a good soldier, but you're needed more at home.

THE END

To follow another path, turn to page 11.
To read the conclusion, turn to page 101.

That's not the last you see of Enoch Crosby. Throughout the war, he sends secret information about British troop movements to the patriots. He relies on you to provide him with a hiding place. You create a special code. Now you recognize Crosby's knock.

Sometimes you even carry messages from Crosby to Mrs. Clark, who runs a small bookshop in town. She's part of the spy network too. You keep secrets during the war. Years later you tell your grandchildren that you helped win the American War of Independence.

THE END

To follow another path, turn to page 11.
To read the conclusion, turn to page 101.

Many young men signed up for the adventure of fighting on a privateer.

CHAPTER 3

Patriot Courage

It is the spring of 1777. It seems as if all the young men in New Milford, Connecticut, are going to war. Many stop by your father's farm to say good-bye. One friend tells you he's going to sea on a privateer. "Privateers hunt and capture British ships," he says. "Lots of our own merchant ships have become privateers. I've already signed on with one. You could find a place too."

You're tempted. You were only 14 when the war began in 1775, but now you are 16. You ask Father for permission to go to war.

41

He can see the determination in your eyes. He hesitates, but then he shakes his head.

Turn the page.

"A sailor's life is not easy. The work is dangerous. It's no life for a farmer like you," Father says.

The next day, you go into New Milford for farm supplies. Some men at the general store tell you that the town is being divided into squads. Each squad must provide a soldier for the Continental army. Many men refuse because they have wives and children to support. Others are too old.

A group of rich storeowners offers you money if you will serve for them. Your father could use the money to hire someone to take your place. But going to sea sounds more exciting.

➴ *To join the Continental army, go to page* **43**.

➴ *To go to sea on a privateer, turn to page* **46**.

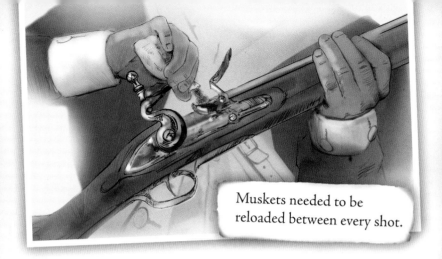

Muskets needed to be reloaded between every shot.

You take the money. It will help your family. You join the 8th Connecticut Regiment at Newtown, Connecticut. An officer leads you and the other recruits to Peekskill, New York, on the Hudson River. Peekskill is a major supply depot.

You spend the summer guarding the supplies and learning how to load a musket quickly. Between each shot, you pour gunpowder into the barrel. You then put a lead ball in the muzzle and shove it down. You put some gunpowder on the pan of the musket and pull back the hammer. It's ready to fire again.

Turn the page.

"If you train hard," the captain says, "you'll get off three shots a minute."

In early September your regiment leaves for Pennsylvania. "The British have taken Philadelphia," your captain announces. "We'll go on to Germantown, Pennsylvania."

On October 4, the captain orders your unit to form a line. "Today we fight. The British are just ahead. Don't fire until you see the buttons upon their clothes!" the captain orders.

But the British begin firing before you are that close. Once the guns and cannons go off, all you see is smoke and fire. Your regiment moves forward. You fire, reload, and fire again, not knowing whether your bullets reach their marks.

Your army pushes the British troops back through their own camp. Then you and your fellow soldiers begin to run out of gunpowder.

The British renew their attack. They shoot at you and charge with their bayonets.

Everyone in your regiment is retreating. You've got no choice but to join them. Amid the noise and shouting, you lose your sense of direction. The grove of trees to the left looks familiar. You head there.

By the time you realize you've turned the wrong way, it's too late. You are face-to-face with a young British soldier. He looks as scared as you are. His gun is aimed at you. Yours is aimed at him. If you shoot, neither of you will miss. You have to think fast.

➻ To fire your musket, turn to page **51**.

➻ To distract the soldier, turn to page **52**.

➻ To surrender, turn to page **56**.

You travel to Bedford Village, Massachusetts. You have an uncle there. It's good to see him. You enjoy a good meal, a good night's sleep, and then you go to the docks. You find Captain Mowry Potter aboard the *Eagle*.

"What do you want?" he asks.

"I'm looking for work on a privateer," you say.

"I'm looking for a cabin boy," he offers.

"But I'm 16, and I want to be a sailor," you say.

"You may be 16, but you're a small fellow. Start as a cabin boy. You need to learn the ropes."

Soon the *Eagle* sets sail. Potter is a harsh master, and the sailors are rough. They take the best of the food and leave the scraps for you. You try to do as the captain asks, but he's quick to scold you for the slightest mistake.

Privateers helped the American Navy battle the British at sea.

Captain Potter cruises along the British coast, looking for British ships. But you don't see a single one. In October 1777, the *Eagle* begins its return journey to Massachusetts.

One day, you spot a tall pole standing alone on the horizon. "Is that land?" you ask an officer.

"Looks more like the bare poles of a ship," he says. He peers through his spyglass. "It's flying a British flag, and it's raising its sails."

Turn the page.

"They are chasing us. Faster, faster!" Captain Potter yells, but you can't get away. In half an hour, the British warship *Sphynx* catches up with the *Eagle*. Its 20 huge guns are aimed at the hull.

"We are taken," a sailor says, hanging his head. "We're as good as dead."

Captain Hunt of the *Sphynx* sends small boats to the *Eagle*. You climb into a boat that takes you back to the British ship. There, sailors toss you a rope. You tie it around your chest so they can haul you up to the ship. Once everyone is aboard the *Sphynx*, the British sink the *Eagle*.

"What a waste," you say.

"If we didn't sink it, we would have burned it," a British sailor says. "We don't need any more supplies."

He notices the buttons on your shirt. They are made of pewter. The motto "Liberty and Property" is engraved on them. "Yankee!" he says with a sneer. He pulls out a knife to snip the buttons away.

"Leave him alone. He's just a boy," a passing British officer growls. You're surprised. The British sailors are kinder to you than the men on the *Eagle*.

The *Sphynx* goes directly to New York, which is under British control. There, the crew from the *Eagle* is sent to the *Asia*, a British prison ship. Supper is a bit of moldy bread and watery soup. There aren't any beds. You sleep on the hard deck wherever you can find room.

One day, some prisoners try to escape by jumping overboard. Two are shot in the water by British guards, but the others make it safely ashore. Their escape gives you hope. You begin to plan your own escape.

Turn the page.

A few days later, a British officer boards the ship. He is looking for a cabin boy for his ship, the *Maidstone*. "You," he says, pointing to a boy named Paul.

But Paul doesn't want to leave his father, who is also a prisoner on the *Asia*. Paul cries and screams. He puts up such a fuss that the officer lets him go.

The officer turns to you. "Do you want to stay here too? The food is better on the *Maidstone*."

➻ *To go with the officer to the* Maidstone,
turn to page **53**.

➻ *To stay onboard the* Asia *and try to escape,*
turn to page **57**.

You fire your musket first. The soldier falls, blood gushing from his head. You fall to your knees and vomit. You've killed a man. You'll have to live with this your entire life — if you survive the war.

You listen. Off to the right, there are voices. They sound familiar. That's the direction you should have gone in the first place. You stand up, wipe your mouth, and run toward the voices.

Turn to page 58.

"Look!" you say, pointing to a distant tree. It's an old trick, but it works. The soldier looks away. You rush forward and knock the musket from his hands. Then you push him down. You're tempted to shoot him, but you resist. The blast might alert his fellow soldiers. You kick him in the stomach. He yelps in pain. Suddenly you hear voices coming from the woods. They sound familiar. You dash in their direction.

Turn to page 58.

You go to the *Maidstone* with the officer, Mr. Richards. You cook his meals and clean his clothes and cabin for him. The *Maidstone* cruises the American coast as far south as Virginia, capturing merchant vessels and sailors. In Virginia, the *Maidstone* captures ships full of tobacco. The money from selling the tobacco will be split among the crew. Even you will get a share.

In December 1777, the *Maidstone* comes alongside a passing British ship. Mr. Richards leans over the rail. "Any news of the war?" he shouts.

Turn the page.

"Burgoyne surrendered at Saratoga in October. The Americans have taken thousands of his men prisoner," a man on the other ship yells.

Burgoyne? No one can believe it. He is one of Great Britain's best generals. His men are highly trained British soldiers.

General Burgoyne's surrender at Saratoga was a turning point in the war.

One spring day while the ship is in New York Harbor, you are allowed to go onshore. It's your first time onshore since you left home. Knowing you are watched, you make no attempt to escape.

Several days later, Mr. Richards sends you ashore again with his laundry. You walk about the city. This time, no one is watching. There's a milk boat at the dock.

The captain of the milk boat is friendly. He has just made a delivery and is returning to Long Island.

"My uncle lives there," you say.

He offers you a ride. "But the British control Long Island. If you're not careful, you'll end up fighting for the British. Or you'll end up dead."

➤ To go to Long Island, turn to page **64**.

➤ To return to the ship, turn to page **66**.

You lift your hands in surrender. "I give up," you say. You refuse to shoot a man at such close range. You're a soldier, not a murderer.

The soldier takes you to the British camp. A few days later, the British march their prisoners to the coast. There, you are put on the prison ship *Asia*. There are hundreds of other patriot soldiers and sailors onboard. The ship begins its journey to New York Harbor.

Every morning, the officer shouts, "Rebels, turn out your dead!" One day, you notice the man sleeping next to you has not moved. You nudge him. He's dead! He either starved or died of disease.

If you're going to survive, you'll have to escape. One dark night, a thunderstorm provides the perfect cover. You wait until a clap of thunder distracts the guards. Then you jump into the icy water of New York's East River and swim. You wait for gunshots, but nothing happens.

You spy a small fishing boat in the distance. It's a long way to shore, and you are not a strong swimmer. The boat is closer. But are the fishermen patriots or Loyalists?

↠ *To swim for shore, turn to page* **63**.

↠ *To head to the boat, turn to page* **65**.

The voices were men from your regiment. You join them on the march toward Philadelphia. "We almost won the Battle of Germantown," one of the men says. "If only we hadn't run out of ammunition . . ." You know that's hopeful thinking. You were outnumbered by the British.

Your regiment marches on without stopping. At last you reach White Marsh, 12 miles north of Philadelphia. You sleep on the soft ground. It's dirtier than a pigsty, and the smoke from the campfires burns your eyes. Supply wagons deliver beef. The cooks roast it over the fire. Your small share is burnt on the outside and raw inside, but you gobble it up eagerly.

One day your captain announces, "General Washington has ordered us to defend the forts on the Delaware River south of Philadelphia. We'll camp at Fort Mifflin and keep the British ships from coming up the river."

You march on toward Fort Mifflin. You spend the first night in a village where the people offer you a good meal and a warm bed. But the next day, you go hungry again. On the third day, you find a goose. By the time it is cooked and divided up, you get one wing. There's no salt or bread to go with it.

In late October 1777, you reach Fort Mifflin. You set up camp and take turns standing guard. An officer takes you aside. "This could be rough," he says. "There are 400 of us trying to hold back the entire British Navy."

A zigzag stone wall makes up one side of the fort. The other sides are half-built stone walls separated by ditches. Cannons line the walls. A small pen between a stone wall and one of the fort's wooden walls is the only safe place.

Turn the page.

More than 150 Continental soldiers died in the Battle of Fort Mifflin.

For five weeks, 12 British ships fire on the fort. The British lob more than 10,000 cannonballs over the fort's walls. After so much bombing, the fort's walls are rubble. There is no protection left.

"We must raise a signal flag to the American ships in the river to the north. They will help us," an officer shouts. He asks for volunteers to raise the flag.

Before you can offer your help, a sergeant volunteers. He climbs to the top of the flagpole and attaches the flag. But as he climbs down, he is hit by British gunfire. He falls to his death.

Soon four or five American ships begin firing on the British. Their help gives you some relief, but it's not enough. The British have won the battle.

That night, you and the rest of the soldiers sneak away. Before you leave, you take one last look at the fort. The area looks as empty as a plowed field.

You have served in the Continental army long enough. It's time to go home. But your captain urges you to be a good patriot and sign up for another year.

➤ *To go home, turn to page* **62**.

➤ *To stay in the Continental army, turn to page* **68**.

You're eager to return to Connecticut. It's a long walk through British territory. One day you pass a farmhouse. You steal six eggs from the barn and grab a shirt and pants off the clothesline. You feel rich! You're not only warmer, but now you look like a farmer, not a soldier.

When you reach New York City, you go to the docks. One of the boats carries milk from Long Island to the city. You tell the captain that your uncle lives on Long Island.

"Would you like a ride?" he offers. If you can reach Sag Harbor, your uncle will help you get home. But it is dangerous. Long Island is also a British stronghold.

→ To go to Long Island, turn to page **64**.

→ To keep walking, turn to page **67**.

You swim to shore. By the time you reach the river's edge, you are exhausted and shivering. There's a man in the distance. "Hello there!" you call. Then you realize that the man is wearing the red coat of a British soldier. He takes you back to the *Asia*.

"Give him 20 lashes," the commander says.

You are tied to a mast, and your bare back is whipped. The whip slashes stripes in your back. Blood runs onto the deck.

Friends drag you away, wipe the blood off your back, and give you water. But you develop an infection and a high fever. Nothing helps. You die a few days later, and your body is dumped overboard.

THE END

To follow another path, turn to page 11.
To read the conclusion, turn to page 101.

Ferries carried people across the East River between New York City and Long Island.

You take the ride to Long Island. It's a long walk to Sag Harbor where your uncle lives. You walk all day. When darkness falls, you find an empty barn and sleep in the hay. Your stomach aches from hunger.

The next morning, an old woman gets water from the well near the barn. Then she goes back to the house. Should you ask her for food? If she's a patriot, she'll help you. If she's loyal to the British, she might turn you in.

→ *To ask for food, turn to page 71.*

→ *To keep moving, turn to page 73.*

Brrr! The cold makes you weak. You head for the boat. "Hello there!" you call, and someone drops a rope into the water.

An old fisherman pulls you aboard. "Where are you headed?" he asks.

"I've got an uncle in Sag Harbor on Long Island," you say.

You stay with the fisherman and his wife for a week. When you are strong enough, you thank them and begin walking. Your uncle's house is 110 miles away. You walk by day and sleep in fields at night. By the third day, you are out of food. You see a farmhouse. You spend the night in the nearby barn. The next day, you're starving. Should you knock on the farmhouse door and ask for food?

→ *To ask for food, turn to page* **71**.

→ *To pass by, turn to page* **73**.

You return to the *Maidstone*. Why risk your life? Mr. Richards has been good to you. You spend the rest of the war on the ship. The officers treat you fairly. The American privateers you've met are far rougher than the British sailors. You've come to believe that the colonists would be better off under British rule.

When the war ends, the Americans gain independence. But you decide to remain on a British ship as a British sailor. You feel more at home on ship than you do on land. And you feel more British than American.

THE END

To follow another path, turn to page 11.
To read the conclusion, turn to page 101.

It's safer to walk, so you keep going. At night, you sleep in barns. You take a fresh shirt and a pair of pants from a clothesline. You rip up a sheet and wrap it around your bare, bleeding feet. Your stomach growls with hunger. You've had nothing to eat but a few chestnuts.

At last you reach familiar country. Now you can safely ask for help. Neighbors welcome you back and give you food, clothing, and a ride home. What joy! You've served your time with the Continental army. From now until America wins freedom in 1783, you serve in the Connecticut militia. You're ready to defend nearby villages and farms if the British attack.

THE END

To follow another path, turn to page 11.
To read the conclusion, turn to page 101.

"I'm a true son of liberty," you say. "I'll stay in the army until the war ends or until I die trying to win it."

A few days before Christmas 1777, you reach Valley Forge in Pennsylvania. General Washington is camped here. You see him walking through camp in his blue uniform. He towers over the other officers. His face is grim.

George Washington was in charge of the troops at Valley Forge.

An officer calls the soldiers together. "We're to begin building huts for winter housing," he says. "General Washington has offered $1 each to the men who finish their hut first."

There are 12 men in your unit. Building a hut without tools is a challenge, but you finish it in two days. You win $1 each!

Now you have a hut, but no blankets, clothes, or shoes. You have a few stools, but the only bedding is straw tossed on the cold, dirt floor.

You don't have much to eat. Most of the time, you live on fire cake. It's made by adding a bit of water to flour and then grilling it over a hot fire.

Your shoes are worn out. On guard duty, you stand on your hat to protect your bare feet. Even so, they bleed and ache from the cold.

Turn the page.

Snow makes travel impossible, but still the soldiers threaten to leave. At night, the chant begins in one hut and travels to the next and the next. "No meat, no coat, no flour, no soldier." Each day you grow thinner.

You wake one morning in February 1778 feeling hot. Has the weather changed? No, you have a fever. Your friends bring you water, but there is nothing else to offer. Your fever grows worse. First you have chills. Then your skin feels like it's on fire. You develop a cough.

"Influenza," the doctor says. "We have no medicine. Keep him warm. Give him water."

But it's not enough. You survived British cannons, but you don't survive the flu.

THE END

To follow another path, turn to page 11.
To read the conclusion, turn to page 101.

You knock on the door and ask for something to eat. "You're not a rebel, are you?" an old woman asks.

"I'm loyal to King George," you lie.

"In that case," she says, "you are welcome to join me for Johnnycakes." She places three of the flattened cornmeal cakes onto a tin plate for you.

As you finish eating, three British soldiers stop by. They look at your empty plate. "Are you feeding rebels too?" they ask the woman.

"Never, sir," she says. "He's as loyal to King George as you are."

"Aye," you say. "It's true. But I must be on my way." They let you go. It was a close call!

Turn the page.

Eventually you find Uncle's house in Sag Harbor. After a few weeks, your uncle arranges for you to take a boat across Long Island Sound to Connecticut under cover of darkness.

It's great to be home. You join the local militia. Your days of fighting with the main army are over. But you help the militia defend Connecticut against several British raids. In that way, you continue to help America win independence in 1783.

THE END

To follow another path, turn to page 11.
To read the conclusion, turn to page 101.

It's safer not to ask. You sneak out of the barn. As you walk, a farmer driving a wagonload of hay pulls up behind you. "Need a ride?" he asks. You hop aboard. When he asks where you are going, you mention your uncle's name.

"He's a good man, a real patriot," the farmer says. He takes you directly to Uncle's house. After a few days, Uncle pays your fare on a boat traveling across Long Island Sound to Connecticut. Your parents are thrilled to have you safely home. "You'll stay?" Father asks.

"Yes," you say. You join the Connecticut militia. If the British attack nearby villages, you're ready and willing to fight. Until then, you work the farm with Father. It feels good to be home.

THE END

To follow another path, turn to page 11.
To read the conclusion, turn to page 101.

British soldiers cut off supplies to the city of Charleston, South Carolina, until the Americans surrendered.

CHAPTER 4

Young Loyalist

It's May 12, 1780, and you live on a plantation near Charleston, South Carolina. Your family is celebrating the surrender of Charleston to the British. In early April, the British began firing on the city. The city was under siege.

On May 11, British General Henry Clinton's guns set fire to several homes. American commander General Benjamin Lincoln and his force of about 5,000 Continental soldiers fought bravely. But the British force was larger and better equipped. Today Lincoln surrendered. The battle for Charleston is over.

Turn the page.

Father is pleased. He's a Loyalist who favors Great Britain. He admires British wealth and power. "They can protect our coastline from outside attack, and they will stop the threat from the Cherokee Indians on the frontier," he says.

"You could go to Charleston," Father says. "It's safely in British hands. And your uncle needs help with his shipping business."

"But I like it here at the plantation," you answer.

"The choice is yours," Father says.

76

➻ *To stay on the plantation, go to page* **77**.

➻ *To go to Charleston, turn to page* **84**.

"I'll stay on the plantation," you say. Your jobs include caring for the horses and checking on the 30 slaves who work on the plantation. When you arrive home from church one Sunday, three slaves are missing.

"I promised not to tell, but they've gone to join the British troops," your little sister says. "They say that any slave who fights for the British can earn his freedom."

"We need those workers," Father says. "When did they leave?"

"Last night."

"It's too late to catch up to them," you say. "Just let them go."

"I hate to do that," Father tells you.

→ To go after the slaves, turn to page **78**.

→ To let them go, turn to page **79**.

You go after the slaves. If you can find them, your father will be pleased with you. You follow a path through the swamp.

Suddenly, someone tosses a net over your head. A gruff voice says, "Caught you, you stinking Loyalist!" You recognize the men as rebels who own small farms nearby. Since the loss of Charleston, rebels hide in the woods. They steal supplies from local farms and attack Loyalists like you and Father.

The rebels tie your arms and drag you to their camp. "We'll teach you a lesson," they say.

"Wait!" one of the men says. "This boy may not share his father's views. Are you a patriot? Or are you loyal to King George?"

⇢ *To say you are a patriot, turn to page* **80**.

⇢ *To tell the truth, turn to page* **81**.

Father finally agrees to let the slaves go. "Perhaps they'll return," he says. "For now, the remaining slaves will have to work harder."

A few days pass. You are working in the barn when your sister comes running. "Four strange men are approaching," she says. "Come quickly!"

You race to the house. Your father and brother have gone to town for supplies. "Be calm," you say to Mother. "Give them food, and they'll go away."

"Take the silver and bury it in the swamp. These men look like thieves," Mother says.

"It's too late," you tell mother. "We'll hide the silver in the attic."

"No, they'll be sure to look there," Mother says. "Please, hide it in the swamp."

⟶ To hide the silver in the swamp, turn to page **86**.

⟶ To hide it in the attic, turn to page **91**.

"I'm a patriot," you lie. "I'll help you."

The men believe you and cut you loose. They tell you that they are part of a militia regiment. They want to prevent the British from winning the rest of South Carolina.

The men plan to raid a nearby plantation for supplies in the morning. You don't want any part of it. You will need to sneak away from them.

You wait until the forest grows dark. When the men fall asleep, you tiptoe away.

Turn to page 82.

It's tempting to lie, but you tell the truth.
"My father's a good man," you say. "If he supports
King George, then so do I."

"Well, then you had better pray that
King George will save you before morning."

The men laugh and drink their rum. Soon
they are snoring beside the campfire. This is the
moment you've been waiting for! You work your
arms free and sneak away.

Rebels often hid in the
woods and attacked
passing Loyalists.

Turn the page.

You don't dare go home in case the men come after you. You steal a horse and set out for Camden, about 120 miles north of Charleston. One of Father's friends, Colonel Zacharias Gibbs, owns a plantation there.

Gibbs is a Loyalist hero. He was captured at the Battle of Kettle Creek in Georgia in 1779. He spent 15 months in a prison run by rebels.

It takes nearly a week to reach Gibbs' home. He welcomes you and asks about Father. You explain what has happened.

"We need men like you fighting to keep this country loyal to Britain," he says.

"I've been thinking of joining the South Carolina Royalists," you say. The colonel nods approvingly. But later, he tells you more about his time in battle and in prison. You realize you might be safer going to Charleston to help your uncle, like your father had suggested.

↠ To go to Charleston, turn to page **84**.
↠ To join the South Carolina Royalists, turn to page **88**.

Charleston, South Carolina, was a busy seaport in 1780.

"Welcome to Charleston," Uncle says. He is a clever businessman who does business with both Loyalists and patriots. Now that the British are in control, business booms. Your uncle signs a note of congratulations to Great Britain's General Clinton. So do 206 others. "That could be dangerous if the British lose this war," you say.

"Don't talk nonsense," Uncle says. "The British won't lose. They have the best-trained army in the world. Their victory here in Charleston is the turning point in this war."

You sign an Oath of Allegiance to the Crown. The oath provides British protection for anyone who signs. Even some patriots sign the oath.

"Don't trust anyone," Uncle warns. "Some people in Charleston are taking supplies to the rebels in the countryside. Watch what you say. They will do anything to destroy the British."

In June 1780, General Clinton rules that all young men must serve in the British militia. Men with more than four children will guard the towns and farms near their homes. You have to serve. You could join a Loyalist horseback, or cavalry, unit. You're a strong rider. Or you could join the South Carolina Royalists, a special regiment formed by South Carolina men to help the British. As a Royalist, you'll be marching on foot.

⇢ *To join the Royalists, turn to page* **88**.

⇢ *To join a Loyalist cavalry unit, turn to page* **89**.

"Fine, I'll take it to the swamp," you agree. You take the bag of silver and rush out the back door just as the men reach the house. They are British soldiers.

"There!" one of them yells. "He's getting away." They chase after you. They think you are a rebel.

"Shoot him!" someone yells.

Bullets whiz past your head. You toss the silver aside and keep running. You stumble when you reach the swamp. A British soldier aims his musket at your head. "Get up," he commands.

The soldier turns away when someone calls his name. If you move quickly, you may be able to escape.

➤ To follow the soldier's orders, go to page 87.

➤ To escape, turn to page 99.

You stand up. The soldier's gun pokes into your back as he leads you back to the house.

Father has returned from town. When he sees you, he roars, "Let my son go! He's no rebel." The soldier lowers his gun.

"You're lucky you weren't shot," Father says after the soldiers leave.

In June 1780, General Clinton orders all young men to serve six months in the British militia. Maybe you'll join the South Carolina Royalists. Loyalist Joseph Robinson formed this group in 1775.

You've also heard of a cavalry regiment forming nearby. This regiment fights on horseback. You are an excellent horseman.

➜ To join the South Carolina Royalists, turn to page 88.

➜ To join the cavalry unit, turn to page 89.

You join the Royalists and help bring order
to Charleston. During the summer of 1780, the
British defeat the rebels at the Battle of Camden
and the Battle of Fishing Creek. You participate in
several raids on rebel farms. Everything goes well
until October, when British troops are defeated at
the Battle of King's Mountain.

You serve the required six months. You're free
to go home. You decide to return to the plantation.

The Battle of Camden
was a major victory for
the British.

Turn to page 98.

Small farms dotted the countryside in Lancaster County, South Carolina.

You grew up around horses and are a good rider. Serving with a cavalry regiment uses your skills. You go to Camden, South Carolina. It's under British control. From there you go to Lancaster County, South Carolina. Captain Christian Huck, a Loyalist lawyer from Philadelphia, is your commander. With Huck in charge, you attack a nearby rebel militia camp at Hill's Ironworks. It is an easy victory.

Turn the page.

On July 12, Huck leads your regiment along with a New York mounted regiment and 35 well-trained British soldiers. You go to William Bratton's plantation. Bratton, a rebel leader, isn't home, so you move to nearby Williamson's Plantation. "We'll find oats for the horses there," Huck says. You fall asleep in a field in front of Williamson's house.

You wake to gunfire. Rebels are attacking. You are half-asleep and confused.

"Run!" Huck yells.

➤ To try to get to your horse, turn to page **92**.

➤ To run to the woods, turn to page **94**.

The men knock on the door. "There's no time," you say. "Take this to the attic!" You hand the bag of silver to your sister. She dashes up the stairs.

The soldiers ask for food. Your mother invites them in. Your cook brings them a hearty meal. When they leave, they say they'll be back.

They return the next day. This time, when they leave, they take several horses, a cow, and chickens.

After they leave, Father says, "We must go into hiding before they come again. It won't be pleasant, but we'll be safe. We'll hide in the swamp."

When your family returns a week later, the house has been torn apart. Valuable paintings are slashed, and the cupboards are empty. The horses are gone. You begin repairing the damage.

Turn to page 98.

Gunfire explodes all around you. Men crumple to the ground. You run to the horses and jump onto the nearest one. "Go!" you yell, slapping it on the rump. The horse bolts forward, taking you to safety. You are lucky. Many Loyalists, including Captain Huck, die at the Battle of Williamson's Plantation.

More defeats follow. In September, your regiment is sent home. There is little hope for a British victory. In October 1781, the final battle of the revolution is fought at Yorktown, Virginia. General Charles Cornwallis, leader of the British forces in the South, surrenders to General George Washington. The war is nearly over, but you are not safe. Loyalists are now threatened by the winning patriots. You must leave South Carolina.

When you arrive home, you find that Mother is eager to leave the war behind. "We have family in Great Britain," she says.

"We'll be safe in East Florida," Father says. "It's a British territory. We'll bring the slaves and begin farming again."

They ask you to help decide.

→ To go to Great Britain, turn to page **96**.

→ To go to East Florida, turn to page **97**.

You run for the woods and take shelter. The fighting is over in 10 minutes. When the shooting stops, 35 Loyalists are dead, including Captain Huck. Another 30 are wounded. The rebels disappear as quickly as they arrived. You return to Williamson's Plantation to help the wounded and bury the dead.

The tide has turned against the British. You are with British troops when they are defeated at the Battle of King's Mountain in October 1780. Another defeat comes at the Battle of Cowpens in January 1781. Your regiment heads home, weary and discouraged. In October 1781, the British surrender at the Battle of Yorktown in Virginia.

In 1782, Congress passes a law to seize Loyalist property. Your father's plantation and your uncle's business will be seized. You decide to leave South Carolina.

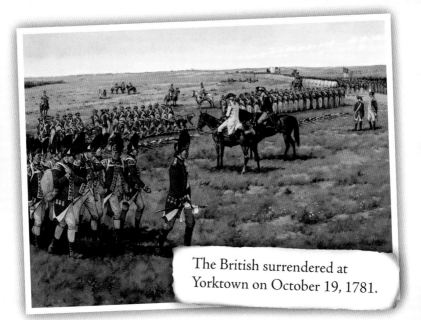

The British surrendered at Yorktown on October 19, 1781.

Many Loyalists are going to Great Britain. "We can start over there," Mother says.

"But if we go to East Florida," Father says, "we can continue farming. I'm a farmer. What would I do in a city? East Florida is a British territory, so we'll be safe there."

↠ *To go to Great Britain, turn to page* **96**.

↠ *To go to East Florida, turn to page* **97**.

You go with your family to Great Britain. It should feel like home. But it doesn't. The cities are too big and noisy. You miss country life.

As a reward for your loyal service during the Revolutionary War, the British government gives you land in Nova Scotia. You move to Canada, and your farm prospers. Over time, you become a respected member of the community.

THE END

To follow another path, turn to page 11.
To read the conclusion, turn to page 101.

You go to East Florida. The population of East Florida grows from about 4,000 to more than 17,000 between 1782 and 1783. However, soon after you arrive, you learn that Great Britain has traded East Florida to Spain in exchange for the Bahamas in the western Atlantic Ocean. The British governor, Patrick Tonyn, assures you that the British government will help you move to a new home. In 1784, you move to the capital city of Nassau in the Bahamas. There, you become a successful businessman. You spend the rest of your life in the sunny Bahamas.

THE END

To follow another path, turn to page 11.
To read the conclusion, turn to page 101.

Your father and brother appreciate your help around the plantation. There is a lot of work to do.

One day a group of rebels shows up. They demand money and supplies. "We have nothing left," Father says.

The soldiers are hungry and angry. They strike Father with a musket. He falls to the ground.

"Leave him alone," you yell. "He's an old man."

"You're not," the soldier says, his voice quiet and calm. He points his gun at you and fires. The blast knocks you off your feet. You feel no pain, but you see blood seeping into the dirt. Is it yours? You feel sleepy and strangely peaceful as you shut your eyes for the last time.

THE END

To follow another path, turn to page 11.
To read the conclusion, turn to page 101.

You leap up and knock the soldier's gun aside.

"Stop, or I'll shoot!" he yells.

You know these swamps and woods better than he does. If you can get out of musket range, you'll be safe. You can hide out here for days or even weeks if you have to.

He fires. You feel a burning at your ear. "It's nothing," you say to yourself. You run faster and faster. Then you stumble forward. The bullet has caused bleeding in your brain. You die in a swamp not far from home.

99

THE END

To follow another path, turn to page 11.
To read the conclusion, turn to page 101.

After the British soldiers left, George Washington (on white horse) led his troops into New York City on November 25, 1783.

CHAPTER 5

Independence at Last

The American Revolution lasted for eight years. During that time, George Washington often ran out of supplies. But he never ran out of men and women willing to fight for independence. More than 200,000 people, including many women and teenagers, participated in the war. They had the advantage of fighting on land they knew and loved.

British soldiers were fighting 3,000 miles from home. It took weeks to bring men and supplies to the battlefield. Communication with leaders in Great Britain took six weeks to three months. British leaders had to make decisions without knowing whether or not King George would support them.

The first major battle of the war was the Battle of Bunker Hill. General William Howe led 2,400 British troops against 1,500 Americans. The Americans, who had built earthworks at the top of the hill for protection, had the clear advantage. But they eventually ran out of ammunition, and the British won the battle. Despite the victory, the British suffered huge losses. Nearly half the British force was killed or wounded. More British soldiers died at Bunker Hill than in any other single battle of the war.

In 1776, Britain tried to take Charleston, South Carolina. They were soundly defeated. But these early losses did not end the conflict. Britain went on to take control of Boston, New York, and Philadelphia. Even Charleston eventually fell to the British in 1780.

The patriots kept on fighting. They won major victories at Trenton and Princeton, New Jersey, and at Saratoga, New York. The final victory came in Virginia at the Battle of Yorktown in October 1781. When Great Britain's General Cornwallis surrendered at Yorktown, the major fighting stopped. In 1782, Great Britain began withdrawing troops and helping Loyalists leave America.

About one-fifth of the American colonists remained loyal to Great Britain. Loyalists lived in every colony, especially in major cities like Boston, New York, and Philadelphia. Some Loyalists remained in their homes after the war, but many moved to Canada, Great Britain, or East Florida, a British territory.

Benjamin Franklin and John Jay traveled to Paris, France, to work out the terms of the peace treaty. The Treaty of Paris was signed on September 3, 1783. As part of the treaty, Britain gave its territory in East Florida to Spain. Many Loyalists who had settled there moved to British-held islands off the American coast.

Once the war ended, the colonies had to develop a national government. They needed a document to lay out the ideas that would guide the nation. In 1787, the U.S. Constitution was written at a Constitutional Convention in Philadelphia. Convention delegates signed the Constitution on September 17, 1787. It then was sent to the states to be approved. In 1790, Rhode Island became the 13th and final state to approve the U.S. Constitution.

George Washington (standing at right) was the first of 39 delegates to sign the U.S. Constitution.

Even before the Constitution was approved, some states demanded changes. Those changes, or amendments, are known as the Bill of Rights. The Declaration of Independence, the Constitution, and the Bill of Rights have guided the United States for more than 200 years.

Time Line

1760 — King George III becomes king of Great Britain.

1765 — British Parliament passes the Stamp Act. Colonists protest the taxes.

1768 — British troops arrive in Boston to enforce laws.

1770 — In the Boston Massacre, British troops kill five colonists.

1773 — Patriots dump tea in Boston Harbor.

1774 — The First Continental Congress meets in Philadelphia.

April 1775 — The first shots of the war are fired at Lexington and Concord, Massachusetts.

June 1775 — The British win the Battle of Bunker Hill.

June 1776 — Patriots defeat the British Navy at Sullivan's Island, South Carolina.

July 4, 1776 — Congress ratifies the Declaration of Independence.

September 1777 — Philadelphia falls to the British; Patriots win the Battle of Freeman's Farm at Stillwater, New York.

October 1777 — British General John Burgoyne surrenders at the Battle of Saratoga; the British win the Battle of Germantown, Pennsylvania.

November 1777 — British troops win the Battle of Fort Mifflin.

May 1780 — Charleston, South Carolina, falls to the British.

August 1780 — The British win the Battle of Camden, South Carolina.

October 1780 — Americans win the Battle of King's Mountain, South Carolina.

January 1781 — Americans win the Battle of Cowpens, South Carolina.

October 1781 — British General Cornwallis surrenders at Yorktown, Virginia.

September 3, 1783 — Leaders from Great Britain and the United States sign the Treaty of Paris.

October 1783 — British troops leave New York.

May 1787 — The Constitutional Convention begins in Philadelphia.

1790 — Rhode Island becomes the last state to approve the U.S. Constitution.

OTHER PATHS TO EXPLORE

In this book, you've seen how the events surrounding the Revolutionary War look different from several points of view.

Perspectives on history are as varied as the people who lived it. You can explore other paths on your own to learn more about what happened. Seeing history from many points of view is an important part of understanding it.

Here are some ideas for other Revolutionary War points of view to explore:

+ Many American Indians sided with the British. They feared the American colonists were moving in to claim the land. What would life have been like for an American Indian during the war?

+ The British encouraged many southern slaves to join British troops. In exchange, the British promised them freedom after the war. What would fighting on the British side have been like for the slaves?

+ The British hired German soldiers, called Hessians, to increase their forces. Most Hessians knew no English. What problems would you have faced as a German fighting on American soil?

READ MORE

Beller, Susan Provost. *Yankee Doodle and the Redcoats: Soldiering in the Revolutionary War.* Minneapolis: Twenty-First Century Books, 2008.

Hall, Margaret C. *The History and Activities of the Revolutionary War.* Chicago: Heinemann, 2006.

Micklos, John. *The Brave Women and Children of the American Revolution.* Berkeley Heights, N.J.: Enslow, 2009.

Ratliff, Thomas M. *How To Be a Revolutionary War Soldier.* Washington, D.C.: National Geographic, 2006.

INTERNET SITES

FactHound offers a safe, fun way to find Internet sites related to this book. All of the sites on FactHound have been researched by our staff.

Here's all you do:

Visit *www.facthound.com*

FactHound will fetch the best sites for you!

GLOSSARY

bayonet (BAY-uh-net) — a metal blade attached to the end of a musket or rifle

gristmill (GRIST-mil) — a building for grinding grain

Loyalist (LOI-uh-list) — a colonist who was loyal to Great Britain during the Revolutionary War

militia (muh-LISH-uh) — a group of citizens who are trained to fight but only serve in time of emergency

musket (MUHSS-kit) — a gun with a long barrel

patriot (PAY-tree-uht) — a person who sided with the colonies during the Revolutionary War

privateer (PRYE-vuh-teer) — a private ship that is authorized to attack enemy ships during wartime

rebel (REB-uhl) — a person who fights against a government

regiment (REJ-uh-muhnt) — a large group of soldiers who fight together as a unit

retreat (ri-TREET) — to move back or withdraw from a difficult situation

BIBLIOGRAPHY

Brown, Wallace. *The King's Friends: The Composition and Motives of the American Loyalist Claimants.* Providence, R.I.: Brown University Press, 1965.

Gundersen, Joan R. *To Be Useful to the World: Women in Revolutionary America, 1740–1790.* New York: Twayne, 1996.

Hawkins, Christopher. *The Adventures of Christopher Hawkins.* New York: New York Times, 1968.

Lambert, Robert Stansbury. *South Carolina Loyalists in the American Revolution.* Columbia, S.C.: University of South Carolina Press, 1987.

Liberty! The American Revolution. DVD. PBS Home Video, 2004.

Martin, James Kirby, ed. *Ordinary Courage: The Revolutionary War Adventures of Joseph Plumb Martin.* Malden, Mass.: Blackwell, 2008.

Raphael, Ray. *A People's History of the American Revolution: How Common People Shaped the Fight for Independence.* New York: Perennial, 2002.

Index